THE NEED TO KNOW LIBRARY™

EVERYTHING YOU NEED TO KNOW ABOUT
STRESS AND DEPRESSION

SABRINA PARYS

Rosen
YA

New York

Published in 2018 by The Rosen Publishing Group, Inc.
29 East 21st Street, New York, NY 10010

Copyright © 2018 by The Rosen Publishing Group, Inc.

First Edition

Library of Congress Cataloging-in-Publication Data

Names: Parys, Sabrina, author.
Title: Everything you need to know about stress and depression / Sabrina Parys.
Description: New York : Rosen Publishing, 2018. | Series: The need to know library | Includes bibliographical references and index. | Audience: Grades 7–12.
Identifiers: LCCN 2017003223| ISBN 9781508174165 (library-bound) | ISBN 9781508174141 (pbk,) | ISBN 9781508174158 (6-pack)
Subjects: LCSH: Stress in adolescence—Juvenile literature. | Depression in adolescence—Juvenile literature. | Stress management for teenagers—Juvenile literature. | Depression in adolescence—Treatment—Juvenile literature.
Classification: LCC BF724.3.S86 P376 2018 | DDC 155.9/042--dc23
LC record available at https://lccn.loc.gov/2017003223

Manufactured in China

CONTENTS

INTRODUCTION... 4

CHAPTER ONE
WHAT CAUSES STRESS IN TEENS? 8

CHAPTER TWO
WHAT CAUSES DEPRESSION IN TEENS?...............................19

CHAPTER THREE
WHAT HAPPENS WHEN WE DON'T
DEAL WITH IT WELL?...32

CHAPTER FOUR
LEARNING TO MANAGE YOUR STRESS AND TREAT YOUR
DEPRESSION..42

GLOSSARY 53
FOR MORE INFORMATION..55
FOR FURTHER READING..58
BIBLIOGRAPHY..59
INDEX 62

INTRODUCTION

The clock is slowly crawling toward midnight. Anna sits in front of her computer staring at a blank Word document. Like many students her age, she is confronted with the dilemma of having too much to do in too little time. Though she had planned to begin her research paper earlier this week, her agenda quickly filled up with other obligations and responsibilities that felt more immediate.

She starts to type but her brain is a million miles away. Why can't I think? I know this stuff. Most of my friends are probably already done with the assignment, she thinks to herself. Looking down at her phone, Anna mindlessly scrolls through her Twitter feed until she realizes that it is after 2 a.m., but she still has a massive amount of work ahead of her. She begins to panic.

Unfortunately, this cycle of sleep deprivation and stress is normal for Anna. Just when she feels caught up in life, something throws her balance off again. Soon enough, she begins to find little enjoyment in her day, and stress becomes an all-too-frequent experience.

Like Anna, many teenagers often find themselves overwhelmed by the demands of life. Trying to find enough time for everything that needs to be done can be exhausting. In fact, a recent "Stress in America" survey conducted by the American Psychological Association (APA) determined that teens between the

Suddenly realizing shortcomings in one's academic performance can cause stress. School is often a frequent cause of stress for many reasons.

ages of thirteen and seventeen are experiencing higher levels of stress than their adult counterparts and that 30 percent of those teenagers even reported experiencing stress-related depression.

While it's true that school can be a significant stressor in a young adult's life, it is often accompanied by other experiences that can cause equal tension, especially when students don't know healthy ways of processing or destressing after going through these experiences. Dealing with the demands and expectations of friends, sports teams, parents, homework, romantic partiners—each competing for attention—can be disorienting when hormonal changes seem to affect every mood. Little things, like a missed appointment or a bad grade, can appear to take on life-or-death proportions.

When stressors like this go unmanaged, teens can find themselves physically and emotionally drained. Often stress arises from short-term problems, but for some teens, stress from one event seems to connect to stress from another, and this cycle can repeat over and over for months or even years. This type of stress, chronic stress, does not necessarily need a specific event to trigger it but instead can be the result of serious situations and circumstances that are mismanaged or too overwhelming to cope with. When chronic stress begins to rule one's life, many young adults may begin to wonder if they are depressed. And, for many teens, depression is indeed more than just a medical term they hear in passing. A toxic home environment, long-term bullying, severe stress, and genetics can all contribute to teen depression. Yet, many young adults ignore symptoms and live with these difficult feelings instead of getting the help they need.

Learning more about how stress and depression work can help a person to make sense of responsibilities and emotions in ways that are healthy and productive. Learning what stress and depression looks and feels like is the first step to healing from it. Temporary stress and long-term stress have different causes and even different means of treatment. Locating what parts of life generate the largest source of frustration can help someone figure out a personalized plan for life-style changes that relieve stress. And knowing how to distinguish sadness from depression and how to get help if someone cannot manage it alone will make for a generally happier life. Increasing knowledge about these complex subjects will help readers to thrive and be comfortable with themselves despite the challenges of their everyday lives.

CHAPTER ONE

WHAT CAUSES STRESS IN TEENS?

Have you ever broken out into a sweat after a pop quiz was announced? Or maybe felt a rush of energy after avoiding an accident? This is the work of your stress hormones reacting to an immediate stimulus. Contrary to what you may assume, stress is a self-preservation trick orchestrated by your body. In small quantities, and during life-threatening situations, the stress reaction is mobilizing and can even save your life. In larger quantities, however, stress can feel overwhelming and frustrating. Learning about the mechanics behind stress can empower someone to understand its complexities.

HOW STRESS WORKS

Stress is a term used in the field of physics to express that pressure is being applied to an object. In 1936, Dr. Hans Selye, a pioneer of human stress research, adapted the term for medicine to describe the feelings and physical reactions that humans have in response to changes or pressures in their environment.

The Mayo Clinic, a nonprofit medical practice and research organization, describes the stress reaction process as an alarm system. When the brain perceives an immediate threat—such as a car swerving toward you—it sounds an alarm notifying the sympathetic nervous system (SNS) that it must ready itself for action. The SNS then dispatches the fight-or-flight response hormones, which prep your body to either fight (react) or flee to safety.

Dr. Hans Selye (January 26, 1907–October 16, 1982) was an endocrinologist who pioneered the study of human stress.

Adrenaline and cortisol are two of these hormones. Adrenaline aids in the production of sweat, increases your heart rate, dilates your pupils, and gives your body a surge of energy. Cortisol, on the other hand, is released slowly and is responsible for regulating functions such as growth, digestion, and the immune system. These hormones work in harmony, helping you respond to imminent danger, which in the case of a car careening toward you means jumping out of the way just in time to avoid getting hit.

GOOD STRESS, BAD STRESS

Not all stress is bad. In fact, stress in small quantities can be beneficial. Eustress, also known as good stress ("eu" meaning "good" in Greek), is light nervousness a person may feel before a job interview or as that person fills out a scholarship application. Light anxiety might accompany these events. But the stress is motivating, not discouraging, and it pushes the person to work hard in order to achieve a goal.

On the other hand, distress, or negative stress, can be triggered by tense situations or events that cause pain or suffering. If parents suddenly divorce, for example, it can be difficult for many teens to overcome feelings of sadness or anger associated with the event. This kind of stress can impact other areas of life and make it harder to focus on everyday demands.

LEVELS OF SEVERITY

A person might encounter many short-term stresses in a given day or week or year, but usually these stresses are not connected. Taking an important test or competing in a big track meet are examples of a short-term or acute stress. For most people, once the event is over, the stress associated with the event often fades away, too.

Long-term stress, or stress that persists day-to-day, can be far more demanding on the body. When teens are faced with longer-term stress, such as feeling pressured to apply to a part-time job, this stress can feel more intense as the feelings of anxiety accompanying the endeavor seem to drag on and on.

When not managed well, long-term stress can often lead to chronic stress. The Centre for Studies on Human Stress tells us that chronic stress is the result of long-term exposure to extreme stress. For many teens, chronic stress can also stem from an inability to manage their minor day-to-day stress. Chronic stress can last years or even decades, severely impacting one's life experience and relation-

Studying for a test can cause good stress, or eustress, and motivate a person to work hard for that good grade.

ships. For example, an undiagnosed learning disability, such as dyslexia, can cause tremendous amounts of stress by virtue of the fact that it is undiagnosed. A teen can spend years in school, frustrated and discouraged at every turn because he or she is unaware that there is an underlying issue contributing to his or her academic distress.

Stress is complex and feels different for everyone, so there is no single solution for combating it. Despite this, everyone can use the methods professionals have designed for managing stress. As with most challenges that teens face, it is important to treat problems as soon as they arise.

STRESS TEST: NORMAL STRESS VS. ABNORMAL STRESS

Stress can quickly feel overwhelming if not managed properly. Taking control of your life means learning how to monitor your feelings and how to place your daily stress into a broader context. It means thinking about stress and the situations that bring it on. Stress tests, or self-evaluation exams, are confidential tools that help you to put your experiences into a clearer perspective. Tools like Mental Health America's online Stress Screener organize a person's stresses into patterns, making it easier to understand how sources of stress are and are not connected to one another and how one's behavior can be a reaction to stress. Approaching stress in this way can make understanding one's feelings a lot easier.

WHAT ARE STRESSORS AND HOW DO THEY AFFECT US?

Stressors, or stress triggers, are things that cause stress. Stressors arise from the circumstances you find yourself in and are therefore unique to each individual. Everyone deals with stress differently. Some people find that they can handle a lot of demands on their time without feeling too overwhelmed, while others may feel immediately uncomfortable when their daily schedules become too packed. Much of how a person deals with stress depends on his or her environment and his or her personality. Nevertheless, no matter who we are or how we function, stressors exist everywhere and can affect anyone. The following are some of the most common stressors facing teens today.

SCHOOL BLUES

According to the "American Time Use" survey conducted by the US Bureau of Labor Statistics, the average American teen spends about 6.8 hours—nearly a third of their day—attending school and participating in educational activities. In fact, the same survey concluded that teens report that their stress levels "far exceed what they believe to be healthy" during the school year.

While it's true everyone deals with the demands of school differently, stressors will inevitably pop up and challenge most of us. Part of school-related stress includes short-term demands like tests and exams. Once the exam is over, the stress of preparing for it fades away as well. However, long-term stressors, such as daunting college applications, can also play a part in the way a teen experiences day-to-day demands. Many teens undertake ambitious schedules, padded with additional responsibilities, in order to appeal to college recruiters. These extracurricular activities, internships, and part-time employment can lead to over-scheduling and can take an adverse toll on the body and mind by creating a never-ending chain of stress each day. Like sticks in a pile, the more sticks one adds, the heavier the pile becomes and the more difficult it is to carry and manage.

BULLYING

While it is easy to assume that the largest stressor related to school is academic, some teens spend sleepless nights worrying about merely getting through a day without being a target of bullying. This kind of stressor can be enormously taxing. Bullying is dangerous and traumatizing—no matter how often it happens and regardless of to whom it is directed. Unfortunately, the prevalence of social media and technology has allowed bullying to migrate into the digital realm, too. Cyberbullying has become a very real stressor in many teen lives. The Pew Research Center reports that 42 percent of teens have had some-one post things about them that they cannot control or change and that 32 percent of teens have been the

targets of "potentially men-
acing" online activity. When
an adolescent's environ-
ment—online or physi-
cal—is a source of fear and
anguish, devastating psy-
chological effects often are
the outcome, with severe
stress, depression, anxiety,
and low self-esteem being
among them.

FOLLOWING
THE CROWD

As a teen, there is always
the temptation to com-
pare yourself to others.
The body undergoes a
tidal wave of hormonal
and physical changes in
the years of adolescence.
When friends begin to

Focusing on schoolwork can seem
difficult when there are many other
concerns fighting for your attention.

date, express sexual desires, or engage in illicit activities, there can be pressure to participate in order to feel
like part of the group. Comparing oneself to others can
also lead to self-esteem or body-image issues that can
have an impact way beyond adolescence. Social circles
can forge a sense of identity for many teenagers, but the
stresses of fitting in or feeling the need to conform may
act as stressors for some young people.

Constantly comparing oneself to others can lead to an unhealthy desire to fit in.

STRESSORS AT HOME

Stressors can appear at home just as quickly as in the outside world. Minor arguments with parents, siblings, or extended family often lead to temporary stress. However, sometimes chronic stress can be the result of complicated family dynamics or circumstances. Some teens experience the hardship of a parent's or loved one's illness. Having to act as a part-time care-giver can be physically, mentally, and emotionally exhausting. Dealing with medications, doctor visits, and picking up extra chores at home may lead to tackling responsibilities that are too demanding for the teenage brain. Other teens can find themselves in the middle of unsavory domestic situations, such as a painful divorce, domestic or verbal abuse, food insecurity, or even homelessness. These are extreme stressors that affect every aspect of a person's ability to function. While it can be easy for some teens to compartmentalize certain stressors in their home life, for many others, serious domestic stress often spills over, affecting their long-term ability to focus and function.

TEENS AND TECHNOLOGY

How much time do you think you spend online? According to Common Sense Media, a nonprofit group focused on the study of teens and technology, the average American teen spends almost nine hours consuming media each day. While technology can be a great source of connection, our widespread dependence on the internet and media can also become a stressor when we do not manage our time well. Left unchecked, constant reliance on digital technologies can turn into digital addiction. Such dependency can make it impossible for a teen to get through the day without being glued to his or her phone or computer. Other important events that require attention, such as school, cultural interests, and friends, fall by the wayside. While the internet can seem like an escape for some teens, dependence on it can lead to many social and real-life problems.

STRESSORS AND TIME MANAGEMENT

Many teenagers feel that they must multitask, or juggle many activities simultaneously, to get through the day. The fact of the matter is that multitasking can be overwhelming, creating a lack of concentration and even procrastination. It is difficult to focus on doing research for an assignment when the temptation to scroll through Twitter is so close at hand. The mind cannot be in two places at once. This conflict causes a lack of concentration that leads to difficulty in completing necessary tasks, which, for most teens, is a common stressor.

For other teens, stress can lead to avoidance. When there seems like too much to do, zoning out with a fun activity such as socializing with friends or binge-watching a TV show may seem like a better use of time than stressing out. However, the inevitable reality of deadlines soon comes crashing down, which then leads to even more stress.

Multitasking can easily lead to distraction that will cause panic when it becomes clear that there isn't enough time to complete a task.

CHAPTER TWO

WHAT CAUSES DEPRESSION IN TEENS?

I n her first and only novel, *The Bell Jar*, poet Sylvia Plath describes her experience with depression as such: "Because wherever I sat—on the deck of a ship or at a street café in Paris or Bangkok—I would be sitting under the same glass bell jar, stewing in my own sour air." It is common for depression to be described like this. The illness can feel hopeless and unrelenting when left untreated. In 2015, the National Institute of Mental Health (NIMH) reported that approximately three million young adults between the ages of twelve and seventeen experienced at least one major depressive episode in the last year. With rates of depression rising in teens and young adults, educating yourself about depression has never been more important.

THE COMPLICATED TRUTH BEHIND DEPRESSION

When we think about depression, many of us associate the illness with feelings of sadness. The stresses

American poet Sylvia Plath (October 27, 1932–February 11, 1963) struggled with depression throughout her life.

of everyday life can sometimes cause us to feel unlike ourselves. But does feeling sad for a few days mean depression? No, not necessarily. It's normal to feel blue after a breakup or to experience irritation after an unusually busy week. Feelings of sadness associated with temporary situations usually pass within a few days. However, for someone with depression, this gloom can permeate every thought and every moment. Sadness may become a defining characteristic of life.

Teens struggling with depression may find it difficult to perform basic functions, like going to school or getting out of bed in the morning. They may begin to lose interest in activities and in people that once brought them joy. Sometimes depression manifests itself as anger, making a person prone to constant irritation or to lashing out at others. In some extreme cases, depression may provoke thoughts of worthlessness, self-harm, and suicidal ideation. The truth of the matter is that depression can feel different for everyone. The common theme that binds all experiences together is that, when left unchecked, depression can be debilitating, all-consuming, and constant.

NATURE VS. NURTURE: WHAT IS RESPONSIBLE FOR DEPRESSION?

There is no single, simple cause of depression. The medical community agrees that many factors can contribute to its development, whether they are biological, environmental, or a combination of both. No matter the reasons for its onset, learning about the complexities of depression will make you better equipped to recognize and handle it.

IT'S NOT ALL IN YOUR HEAD

Depression is somewhat genetic, meaning that it can run in families and that carrying certain genes can make someone predisposed to developing depression. But it's important to note that evidence of these genes does not mean someone's fate is predetermined. Many people who have the genes never develop depression. Likewise, many people without the genes may still be vulnerable to depression. Genes are just one spoke on a wheel of possible influences.

When we talk about the biology of depression, the term "chemical imbalance" often comes to mind. But

Some health conditions, like depression, can run in the family. Scientists are not yet sure about the strength of the links between genes and depression.

describing depression in terms of chemicals is a simplistic way of talking about depression, as the illness is much more complicated and varied. When a teen becomes depressed, neurotransmitters, chemicals that carry messages from one nerve cell to another, may communicate the wrong thing or not enough of it. When neurotransmitters that regulate mood malfunction, sometimes medication is prescribed to bring the body back into balance. Scientists are still studying the links between chemicals and depression in human beings.

STRESS AND DEPRESSION

The amount of stress a teenager encounters and how he or she deals with it can influence depression. Although stress and depression are not always related, the two can certainly feed into each other when severe stress becomes a key component in a person's mental health struggles.

Kidshealth.org, the Nemours Foundation online mental health resource, also points out that the brain is still developing during adolescence. Hormones communicate information about growth, mood, and social skills, and this process affects a teen's behavior and reasoning skills. When a young adult is exposed to too much severe stress or engages in activities that impact cerebral development, such as drinking or drugs, the brain's delicate chemistry is thrown off balance. In some cases, this imbalance can induce depression.

EXTERNAL CAUSES

One's environment can have a profound impact on one's personality, outlook, and one's ability to cope with stressors. If a teen is always criticized by a parent or made to feel inadequate by peers, he or she will internalize feelings of self-consciousness and low self-esteem. This type of negativity, reinforced regularly, can

The way that a parent or loved one criticizes, pressures, or misunderstands a teen can cause that teen to feel overwhelmed with stress.

increase the likelihood of developing depression in some young adults.

For many teens, the reality of an unstable home life affects their day-to-day outlook. When basic living needs are difficult to meet on a regular basis, a teen can experience poverty, homelessness, or food insecurity. Having to worry about when a next meal might come or how he or she will be able to afford basic needs can take years off a teen's life. Likewise, observing negative ways of coping with stress from close family or friends leads many teens to assume the same toxic habits.

Psychologists also point out that many severe stressors from other environments, such as school, leave their marks on a person's psyche as well. When teens find themselves the target of bullying on a daily basis, they can grow to fear an environment that is supposed to keep them safe. When no one steps in to intervene or the person being bullied does not seek outside help, feelings of extreme depression or helplessness grow.

TRIGGERS AND TRAUMA

Major life events, such as death or trauma, sometimes trigger depression. Grieving for a loved one is an extremely challenging and painful process. The days and months following his or her death can be colored by uncontrollable anger or despair. Adjusting to a new routine or domestic situation can take time and patience. While many teens eventually find a way of coping with their feelings, for some this process can become unmanageable, leaving them unable to return to reality. Other equally traumatic experiences such as sexual assault or domestic violence can leave teens with an impaired sense of self-worth and severe stress. Feelings of guilt, confusion, anger, and self-loathing can accompany this experience. The inner turmoil one feels as a result of trauma may result in depression if left unchecked.

WHAT DOES DEPRESSION LOOK LIKE?

There are many types of depression. Episodes, or

periods of intense depression, can be brought on by something as simple as the weather or as complex as genetics. For example, people who suffer from seasonal affective disorder (SAD) experience recurrent depression, which most commonly starts in the fall and lasts through the winter season—or it may afflict sufferers between the late spring through the summer. Depressive periods, of course, can get better with time and help, but the severity or frequency of episodes can be indicative of major depressive disorder (MDD). According to the Diagnostic and Statistical Manual of Mental Disorders (DSM-V), a text used by psychiatrists to diagnose mental illness, a person with MDD experiences bouts of depression, each lasting at least two weeks, accompanied by at least five major symptoms of depression. Another type of depression, persistent depressive disorder (PDD), describes depression that lasts two years or longer.

Because depression can encapsulate such a broad spectrum of experiences, it can also be related to things such as a menstrual cycle, substance abuse, and medication.

Depression can even be a symptom of another medical condition. When a person is diagnosed with bipolar disorder, his or her depression is part of a cycle of highs and lows. A person with bipolar disorder will often feel waves of manic activity, characterized by high, frenzied energy, followed by a period of deep, depressive gloom. Teens diagnosed with other mood or anxiety disorders may also experience depression as a side effect or symptom of that condition.

Sharing your feelings, experiences, and outlook with a medical professional is one of the best ways to figure out what help you need.

While a medical doctor is the only one who should ever formally diagnose depression, there are emotional, behavioral, psychological, and physical symptoms that you can look out for. The following list outlines some common symptoms or thoughts that may point toward depression:

- Feelings of constant despair or emptiness
- Crying more easily and frequently
- Frequent headaches or unexplained physical pains
- Trouble concentrating or staying on task
- Social isolation or lack of participation in events that used to bring enjoyment
- Exhaustion and fatigue
- Constant anger or irritation that seems difficult to place
- An inability to sleep or stay asleep, or sleeping too much
- Overwhelming anxiety or guilt
- Recurring thoughts of suicide or self-harm

WHOM DOES DEPRESSION AFFECT?

Something that makes depression and other mental illnesses difficult to talk about is the stigma that surrounds them. Many people believe, falsely, that mental illness is a sign of weakness or abnormality. While society is debunking this myth more and more frequently, many people still feel shame about mental illness and even avoid seeking help for fear of being judged or stereo-

CELEBRITY CASE STUDY

What do Nicki Minaj, Selena Gomez, Miley Cyrus, the Rock, and Lady Gaga have in common? Aside from being celebrities, they are people who deal or have dealt with depression.

Some people live with depression and say nothing about it, even to close friends. While everyone may not want to discuss their mental health, when people are silent, they stigmatize mental illness instead of validating that it is a common problem. It can be hard to accept something that popular culture is not comfortable discussing.

But celebrity puts a person in the unique position of having a powerful platform that can be used to provoke an active conversation about mental illness. It is often the case that celebrities take advantage of that position. Lady Gaga, for example, established her Born This Way Foundation to spread awareness about and encourage kindness toward topics such as mental illness, harassment, and bullying.

typed. The fact is, depression is nobody's fault. The more people learn about mental health, the more they realize that depression can and does happen to anyone—and that it's nothing to be ashamed about.

Current research suggests that certain groups of people can be more vulnerable to depression because of circumstances such as environment, gender, age, or

Depression does not discriminate between cultures or genders. But there are certain environmental factors that make some groups more likely than others to become depressed.

other medical conditions. For example, NAMI tells us that women are 70 percent more likely to experience depression than men and that people who identify as part of the LGBTQ community may be more vulnerable to depression because of the discrimination they face on a wider spectrum. While data helps us to make sense of the far-reaching effects and patterns of subjects such as mental illness, it is unwise to assume that someone is destined to experience depression just because he or she seems to fit a model.

MYTHS AND FACTS

MYTH: Sadness is the only symptom of depression.

FACT: Depression is a complicated illness that affects the brain, the behavior, and the outlook of those suffering from it. While chronic, or persistent, sadness can be a primary symptom of depression, it is certainly not the only indicator. People with depression can show signs of irritability, anger, anxiety, and physical illnesses.

MYTH: Stress is unavoidable; there is no reason to plan for it.

FACT: Stress is a predictable part of life. But learning how to manage, plan, and deal with it can significantly decrease the pressures of day-to-day activities.

MYTH: Stress can be caused only by negative experiences or events.

FACT: According to the National Institute of Mental health, stress is the "brain's natural reaction to any demand." Stress can, in fact, be caused by a multitude of events or feelings—positive or negative.

CHAPTER THREE

WHAT HAPPENS WHEN WE DON'T DEAL WITH IT WELL?

When we ignore problems, it can feel like we are sitting on a broken chair hoping it won't collapse beneath us. For many teens, serious stress and alarming depression often go unmanaged and untreated. In this chapter, we'll explore what the symptoms of stress overload, stress mismanagement, and depression often look and feel like.

SYSTEM SHUTDOWN: I CAN'T HANDLE IT ALL

When someone is exposed to prolonged stress, the stress response can go into panic mode and refuse to shut down. When this happens, the nervous system continues pumping stress hormones into the body at high rates. While these hormones are meant to give you energy in immediate danger, their constant presence in the body gives our systems little opportunity to relax and rest. Being on high alert all the time takes a toll on the body, resulting in frequent headaches, intense

Prolonged stress can take a physical toll on the body. But the relationship between stress and the body is not always clear.

stomach pains, and trouble sleeping. This is what we call stress overload. Following are some additional symptoms and signs that might point toward a body in overdrive:

- Trouble falling or staying asleep
- Racing thoughts, worries, or anxieties
- Difficulty remembering things
- Always feeling tired or lethargic
- Headaches or stomach pains become routine
- Feeling sick more often than usual; loss or increase of appetite

- Inability to focus or concentrate
- Consuming feelings of sadness or depression
- Sudden and extreme anger

These symptoms are not mutually exclusive. It's notable that they are mostly symptoms that aren't easy to see, although someone experiencing them might be vocal about these sensations. Those that require pattern recognition are probably more likely to be noticed by the sufferer.

When we do not find ways to manage our stress, its buildup in our lives can take on the role of a cavity: stress can become a painful ache that can spread and worsen if we ignore it. As with any issue rooted in psychology, chronic stress can cause severe emotional strain and can breed a different long-term issue. For example, substance abuse, eating disorders, anxiety disorders, anger, and depression can all be the result of unchecked chronic stress. Surefire physical signs that stress may be too overwhelming to handle are frequent panic attacks, shortness of breath, racing thoughts, severe anxiety, or anxiousness. Though depression and stress are not always related, they certainly can flow into each other.

WHAT HAPPENS WHEN DEPRESSION GOES UNTREATED?

Many people suffering from depression do not realize that their suffering is not normal. People can spend years

HINDSIGHT IS 20/20: DOCUMENTING STRESS PATTERNS & TRIGGERS

Finding patterns is what science is all about. When something happens more than once, it's possible that it may be part of a trend or phenomenon and that realization can have a greater importance. When you find yourself stressed out, take a moment to write down how you feel and what triggered your emotions. The more rigorously you document your stress, the more clearly you will be able to connect point A (your stress) to point B (your stressor). When a relationship or a correlation emerges, this awareness can empower you to address your triggers and face your stress head-on.

Being proactive about documenting your stress empowers you to control it better. It's easier to solve a problem with a clear cause.

internalizing their emotions or blaming themselves for their damaging thoughts or behaviors, often never considering the fact that their condition is an illness that they can get help to overcome. When they do not heed the symptoms of depression, those symptoms become more serious and more difficult to overcome. In fact, the Centers for Disease Control and Prevention (CDC) explains, "just experiencing one episode of depression places an individual at a 50 percent risk for experiencing another episode, and further increases the chances of having more depression episodes in the future."

NUMBING THE PAIN

The pain of depression can be distressing enough that many people often look for ways to self-medicate. For many, the temptation to seek escape through alcohol, drugs, or even food can seem like an easy fix for complicated problems, acting as a temporary release of the pressure they regularly face. However, what many fail to realize is that the fix is only temporary, and it treats a symptom instead of the cause.

The National Institute for Drug Abuse (NIDA) tells us that drug use can "tap into the brain's communication system and tamper with the way nerve cells normally send, receive, and process information." For instance, using drugs like cocaine trick the reward pathway in the brain in ways that can induce dependency. Where cocaine also has the function of stimulating the brain, depressants like alcohol slow down the brain's activity, causing a sensation of loosened inhibitions.

Turning to substances as a coping mechanism or as an avoidance tactic is not only illegal and dangerous but also always fails to solve the problem. The American College of Pediatrics states that high-risk behavior can have a deep impact on the developing teenage brain because the neural connections that often lead to addiction and dictate emotional well-being are still being formed. The abuse of drugs or alcohol can affect a teen's devel-

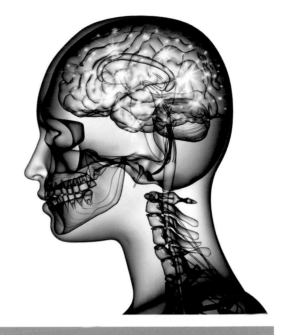

Unhealthy coping habits can rewire important connections in the brain and make depression worse or more ingrained.

oping brain in ways that can reinforce depression and addiction. What's worse is that, with the brain rewired for depression and addiction, a teen can carry these issues with them into adulthood.

COMFORT FOOD

Another form of escapism often accompanying depression is taking refuge in food. Food can be a comfort in difficult times, but for some people, overeating becomes a way of coping with or ignoring their feelings of depression. The long-term consequences of such behavior are damaging, both physically and psychologically. Significant weight gain can lead to obesity, eating disorders, high cholesterol, heart problems, diabetes, and physical ailments such as shortness of breath, decreased stamina, and chronic pain—all of which may contribute to already mounting stress and depression.

EVERY DAY BECOMES A CHALLENGE

"What's the point of even trying?" or "I'm such a loser. No wonder no one likes me": These are common

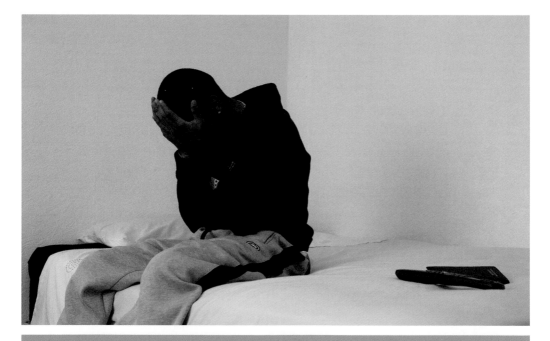

Severe stress in conjunction with depression can lead to despairing thoughts with serious implications for one's emotional well-being and health.

thoughts that cloud the reality of someone with serious depression. When these despairing thoughts become a refrain in someone's mind, it is incredibly difficult to mute them or see past them. Critical thinking, when coupled with depression, can cast a wide net and sometimes lead a person to a crisis point. Unfortunately, for many this can mean resorting to self-harm or thinking about suicide. According to the APA, suicide is third in the leading causes of death in the age group of fifteen-to-twenty-five-year-olds. Untreated depression is among one of the more severe risk factors that can contribute to this statistic. If you or someone you know is exhibiting extreme signs of depression, it's important to get into contact with a hotline, crisis center, or medical professional right away. Suicide is preventable, and depression is treatable. There is no reason why these thoughts should be suffered alone.

TEN GREAT QUESTIONS TO ASK A GUIDANCE COUNSELOR

1. Given that my friend's parents seem to be the main source of her constant anxiety, whom should she talk to about her stress?
2. All I can think about—night and day—is getting into a good college. The pressure of being the perfect candidate is affecting my concentration in school and at home. What can I do to alleviate the academic stress I feel?
3. More often than not, I find myself wanting to be alone. When I come home from school, I have little motivation to do my homework or to interact with other teens my age. Should I be concerned about feeling this way?
4. My friend is often gloomy: she barely talks to anyone, sits alone at lunch, and makes comments about the pointlessness of life. Is she just being a teenager, or are her actions indicative of something serious like depression?
5. I find myself wanting to be involved in a lot of activities and after-school social gatherings—I never want to feel like I'm missing out on anything. But recently, I feel tired all the time and can't focus on getting basic things done. How can I feel involved without feeling burned out?

6. My family is struggling financially so I have begun a part-time job to help as much as I can. My responsibilities at work and at school are starting to collide and stress me out. What should I do?
7. I don't think I'm depressed ... I just feel angry all the time. Everything that happens seems to annoy me for some reason. Is this normal?
8. I always come home with the intention of working on my homework, but I end up spending my whole day on social media. Later at night, I find it hard to catch up on all my work. How can I learn to better manage my time?
9. My classmates often make fun of me and make me feel worthless. I stay awake at night and feel anxious about going back to school every day. What can I do?
10. Can you recommend some useful resources that will help me to learn how to manage stress or overcome my depression?

LEARNING TO MANAGE YOUR STRESS AND TREAT YOUR DEPRESSION

When dealing with too much stress or depressive feelings, it may feel like there is no end in sight. The best way to treat severe stress and manage depression is to reach out to a counselor, a trusted adult, or your primary care physician to address your concerns and feelings. No advice, whether gleaned from this book or a good friend, can ever make up for the guidance of a medical professional. There are many other ways that you can supplement a healthy lifestyle, however. Learning stress management techniques, building a healthy perspective on life, and assuming practical strategies and coping mechanisms can help you to weather the day-to-day stresses life or depression throws at you.

GUARDING YOUR BODY AGAINST STRESS

Taking proper care of your body can help you to fight off stress. One of the best ways to keep your brain healthy is to make sure you are getting enough rest.

Getting enough rest is an investment in one's mental and physical health. And it improves school performance.

The National Sleep Foundation (NSF) recommends that teens get at least 8 ½ to 9 ½ hours of sleep each night. Yet, busy schedules, early school start times, and changes in the circadian rhythm associated with adolescence prevent many teens—almost 87 percent—from getting enough rest each night.

Many teens try to counteract sleep deprivation experienced during the week by binge-sleeping during the weekend. This practice, however, does nothing to bring one's rest up to speed—it only works to further confuse the body's sleep rhythms. Insufficient sleep can lead to impaired judgment, lowered concentration, dependency on caffeine, insomnia, increased stress, and irritation. Taking the time to establish a sleep routine and learning how to stick to it can significantly aid in your ability to approach stress with a clear head. Banning screens, technology, and other media from the bedroom is a great first step in ensuring a quiet sleep environment. Reading, listening to relaxed music, meditating, and keeping your room dark and cozy are just a few suggestions that can also enhance the quality of your rest.

GET MOVING!

Diet and exercise have a huge impact on a person's ability to deal with stress. When coupled with a well-balanced diet of vegetables, fruits, whole grains, and protein, exercise can help the body to meet the challenges and stresses it might encounter. However, the 2016 United States Report Card on Physical Activity for Children and Youth released by the National Physical Activity Plan Alliance tells us that only 21 percent of youth in America meet the physical activity guidelines that the plan outlined. It is not always a priority for adults to encourage kids to engage in the recommended sixty minutes of exercise each day, even though doing so can maintain health, strengthen bones, increase dopamine levels, and promote a lifetime of good health habits. It is as easy as taking a walk and can be as fun as participating in a group activity like sports. It is essential that people are taught at a young age to recognize that a well-balanced mind means a well-balanced body.

Staying active and exercising is an essential part of wellness. It's even more fun with friends.

LEARNING HOW TO PRIORITIZE

A large part of effective stress management is learning how to structure your time and approach your problems. For many teens, it can be easy to default to avoiding responsibilities because watching TV or spending time online can seem like a welcome distraction when there is a lot of tough work to be done. Eventually, though, the responsibilities that one ignores cannot be ignored any longer. This realization can cause panic and extreme distress.

Healthychildren.org, an online health resource sponsored by the American Academy of Pediatrics, urges teens to tackle problems and responsibilities head-on. However, it can seem tough to know where to start when your to-do list is constantly growing. Learning how to integrate management techniques into your life can take some practice. Once these habits become second nature, they can save you time and prevent frustration.

DIVIDE AND CONQUER

An easy way to approach your responsibilities is to learn how to prioritize by ranking your tasks based on level of importance. Once you have decided that science homework is more important to complete than an art project, it becomes easier to focus on the task at hand. Learning how to prioritize can also mean scheduling recurring tasks. What are your daily, weekly, and monthly obligations and tasks? Are some things more important than others? Are tasks involving school more important than tasks involving friends? Can you afford to drop less important tasks? Could you create a schedule that takes these activities into account? These are all questions that will help put your responsibilities into perspective.

For bigger, more daunting responsibilities, it is helpful to break a project into smaller parts. Let's say you have a big paper due in two weeks. Plan your approach to the task in sections rather than attempting to tackle the whole paper in one day. For example, you could spend one day doing research, another day organizing your research, the next day making an outline, the following day drafting a copy of your paper, and subsequent days editing and improving it. This way a task doesn't seem too overwhelming or tough to handle, and you can work on multiple unrelated tasks so that you don't get fatigued from staring at one of them.

A BALANCING ACT

Sometimes we find that no matter how well we manage our time, it still seems like we can't get everything

Making lists, staying organized, and reviewing commitments can help you to stay on top of balancing all the stress of life.

done. Part of managing stress also means acknowledging when you are stretched too thin. So many of us feel that we must accept every opportunity that comes our way. This can make us lose sight of our long-term goals. It also adds pressure to existing stress. It's smart to periodically review your commitments and your relationships, especially if you constantly feel burned out. Knowing when to say no, whether to a social invitation or an extracurricular activity, is a valuable skill that will help maintain a healthy balance.

It's equally important to make time for the things you love. Stress can be abated when we take the time to relax and recharge. Making the time to develop a hobby, to read, to take a walk, to write in a journal, or even just to have a silent moment to yourself is an important part of a balanced lifestyle. Making time for fun can help lower stress levels as well. Managing stress, believe it or not, can actually be easier when we don't lose sight of the things, people, and activities that bring us joy.

GETTING TREATED FOR DEPRESSION

The most difficult part of treating depression is the first step: asking for help. Connecting with a school counselor, a trusted adult, or your primary care physician is the best way to start managing depression seriously. As with stress, do not fall into the trap of ignoring signs or rationalizing symptoms. The sooner you ask for help, the sooner you will start to gain control of your depression and your life.

SPOTLIGHT ON RESOURCES

Healthychildren.org offers teens a My Personal Stress Plan worksheet that can help readers workshop a problem and formulate a strategy to effectively deal with stressors they are experiencing.

The Nemours Foundation website, TeensHealth, offers a Stress and Coping Center resource, which aims to answer questions readers have about the different aspects that stress plays in daily life.

Erika's Lighthouse, a not-for-profit organization dedicated to spreading knowledge about teenage depression, offers teens a free depression screening test and a Depression Toolbox. It provides readers with resources and information about understanding and treating depression.

Like chronic stress, depression is as unique as the person carrying it. It comes from a blend of life circumstances, personal history, and genetics. Therefore, treatment often requires a dynamic approach. Medication might be a helpful treatment for one person, while psychotherapy, or talk therapy, might be most effective for another. Because depression is often the result of both environment and biology, a combination of approaches that tackle it from the inside and the outside are sometimes necessary. Depending on the type and depth of depression being experienced, a medical professional might suggest one, the other, or both. Make sure to discuss the pros and cons of each approach with your psychiatrist in order to figure out a plan that might work best for you.

GETTING CREATIVE AND STAYING ACTIVE

Keeping your body and mind active are not just things that apply to beating stress. They apply just as much to depression. Staying on your feet and engaging in creative outlets can help keep depression in check. While exercise alone cannot treat severe depression, regular aerobic activity has been shown

Stress and depression are not burdens one should carry alone. Counselors and licensed professionals are great people to consult when overwhelmed.

to help people with mild depression by increasing serotonin levels in the brain. After a long jog or other intense activity, the brain floods with endorphins, which researchers have proved elevate one's mood. This is known as the runner's high. Introducing physical activity into your schedule can be a productive way of channeling your energy.

Likewise, adopting hobbies, pursuing creative projects, or engaging in volunteer work can do wonders. You might divert the energy that you normally use to criticize yourself or to feel blue toward painting, writing, reading, learning a new skill, or even helping others.

SHARING THE BURDEN

A healthy support network of friends and family can be a great way to talk about and work through your emotions. Managing depression often means dealing with the various lows and highs one experiences throughout the length of a given episode or phase. Surrounding yourself with empathetic friends, understanding loved ones, and a therapist with whom you really connect are all great ways of sharing and relieving the burden of depression. While you may feel hesitant to share your feelings, you might be surprised at how often a simple conversation with another person can lighten your load or adjust your perspective.

THE ROAD AHEAD: STAYING POSITIVE ABOUT STRESS AND DEPRESSION

Have you ever noticed that often the most optimistic people you know seem to be the happiest? Much of the way you look at life affects the way you handle it. Boxing legend Muhammad Ali had this to say about perspective: "Often it isn't the mountains ahead that wear you out, it's the little pebble in your shoe." Perspective can have a large influence on the way we tackle problems. Your behavior and your attitude can be easily influenced by the type of thoughts you allow yourself to have. Focusing on the negative—the pebble in our shoe—can hide the positive aspects of life right in front of us. When we keep an open mind, on the other hand, and look toward life with enthusiasm, daily demands become a whole lot less distressing. The most important thing you can do—whether you are battling depression or encountering stress—is to focus on your victories, as small as they may seem, and to remain positive about the brightness of the future.

GLOSSARY

acute stress Intense stress, usually brief in duration, that is often caused by a difficult event.

binge-sleeping Sleeping more than one usually does in a short span of time.

bipolar disorder Depression characterized by two extremes: periods of greatly exciting highs and incredibly draining lows.

caregiver A person responsible for the well-being of someone with an illness or disability.

chronic stress Severe stress that is often the result of long-term stressors.

cyberbullying Bullying that occurs online and may involve one or many strangers or acquaintances.

depressants Substances that slow down the central nervous system, with side effects that include sluggishness and a sensation of relaxation.

digital addiction A compulsive dependence on digital technology that can negatively impact a person's relationships and performance in school and work.

distress A type of stress caused by being overwhelmed with a positive event or the presence of negative events or occurrences.

dopamine A hormone released by the brain in response to a stimulus that causes good feelings.

episodes A distinct instance of depression or some other recurring affliction.

eustress Often called "good" stress, it indicates a type of stress that motivates a person without overwhelming them; it is a positive response to a stressor.

fight-or-flight response A response to stimuli judged stressful or dangerous. The sympathetic nervous system secretes adrenaline and cortisol to help the body act instantly to perceived threats.

major depressive disorder (MDD) Episodes of depression lasting at least two weeks and accompanied by at least five major symptoms of depression listed in the DSM-5.

neurotransmitters Chemicals that carry messages from one nerve cell to another.

overscheduling Being responsible for more activities than one can perform.

seasonal affective disorder (SAD) A type of mood disorder characterized by recurrent episodes of depression that are often related to seasonal changes in weather.

self-medicate Attempting to treat, relieve, or avoid symptoms of stress or depression without consulting a professional.

stereotype When many people assume that every individual in a group shares a uniform and narrow set of traits.

stigma A condition or behavior that is associated with shame.

stress overload A condition in which the body begins to fail to sustain stress levels over a long period of time, with symptoms that include headaches, sleeplessness, and racing thoughts.

sympathetic nervous system (SNS) Part of the nervous system that controls your immediate reactions to stress through physiological means.

FOR MORE INFORMATION

The American Institute of Stress (AIS)
6387B Camp Bowie Blvd #334
Fort Worth, TX 76116 USA
(682) 239-6823
Website: http://www.stress.org
This institute aims to provide the public, health care
    professionals, and diverse communities with the
    knowledge to combat and manage stress in daily
    life. The website offers comprehensive research on
    the topic of stress and resources that can help read-
    ers to assess, learn, and manage their stress.

American Psychological Association (APA)
750 First St. NE
Washington, DC 20002-4242
(800) 374-2721
Website: https://www.apa.org/topics/index.aspx
This association is America's largest organization of
    psychologists and mental health professionals. Their
    website offers extensive information about men-
    tal health topics, a psychological help center, and
    advice on the topic of choosing a psychologist or
    mental health provider.

Canadian Mental Health Association (CMHA)
2301-180 Dundas Street West
Toronto, ON M5G 1Z8
Canada
(613) 745-7750

Website: http://www.cmha.ca

This association is dedicated to being an advocate, an educator, and a resource for those struggling with mental illness. The website offers an abundance of information about mental health topics and provides visitors with resources, such as brochures, links to local CMHA branches, and mental health advice.

Mental Health America (MHA)
500 Montgomery Street, Suite 820
Alexandria, VA 22314
(800) 969-6642
Website: http://www.mentalhealthamerica.net

This grassroots organization is dedicated to teaching and treating mental illness. The organization offers free online mental health screenings, an easy-to-use database for finding local affiliates, and an extensive resource page.

Mental Health Commission of Canada
350 Albert Street, Suite 1210
Ottawa, ON K1R 1A4
Canada
(613) 683-3755
Website: http://www.mentalhealthcommission.ca

This organization is dedicated to forwarding mental health literacy and affecting health care policy change through resources, studies, strategy, and outreach. Access webinars, resources, and find out more about mental health in Canada on their website.

National Alliance on Mental Illness (NAMI)
3803 N. Fairfax Drive, Suite 100
Arlington, VA 22203
(800) 950-6264
Website: http://www.nami.org
This alliance is dedicated to the discussion, prevention, and treatment of mental illness in America. The
   website offers teens, parents, adults, and educators
   readily available resources, information, and hotlines
   on various topics of mental illness.

WEBSITES

Because of the changing nature of internet links, Rosen
Publishing has developed an online list of websites
related to the subject of this book. This site is updated
regularly. Please use this link to access this list:

http://www.rosenlinks.com/NTKL/stress

FOR FURTHER READING

Desetta, Al. *Pressure: True Stories by Teens About Stress.* Minneapolis, MN: Free Spirit Publishing: 2012.

Harmon, Daniel. *Frequently Asked Questions About Overscheduling and Stress* (FAQ: Teen Life). New York, NY: Rosen Publishing, 2010.

Hipp, Earl. *Fighting Invisible Tigers: Stress Management for Teens.* Minneapolis, MN: Free Spirit Publishing: 2014.

Lin, Y.S. *Defeating Depression* (Effective Survival Strategies). New York, NY: Rosen Publishing, 2016.

Owens, Michael, and Amy Gelman. *I'm Depressed. Now What?* (Teen Life 411). New York, NY: Rosen Publishing, 2012.

Peterson, Judy Monroe. *Frequently Asked Questions About Antidepressants* (FAQ: Teen Life). New York, NY: Rosen Publishing: 2010.

Porterfield, Jason. *Teen Stress and Anxiety* (Teen Mental Health). New York, NY: Rosen Publishing, 2014.

Spencer, Ann. *I Get Panic Attacks. Now What?* (Teen Life 411). New York, NY: Rosen Publishing, 2012.

Staley, Erin. *Defeating Stress and Anxiety* (Effective Survival Strategies). New York, NY: Rosen Publishing, 2016.

Way, Jennifer, and Sarah Van Duyne. *What Can Your Do About Stress and Anxiety?* (Contemporary Diseases and Disorders). New York, NY: Enslow Publishing, 2015.

Wroble, Lisa A. *Dealing with Stress: A How-to Guide.* Berkeley Heights, NJ: Enslow Publishers, 2012.

BIBLIOGRAPHY

American Institute of Stress. "Definitions." Daily Life, Oct. 3, 2016. http://www.stress.org/daily-life.

American Psychiatric Association. "Depressive Disorders." Diagnostic and Statistical Manual of Mental Disorders, 5th Edition. Arlington, VA: American Psychiatric Publishing, 2013.

American Psychological Association. "Stress in America™: Are Teens Adopting Adults' Stress Habits?" Retrieved August 20, 2016. http://www.apa.org/news/press/releases/stress/2013/stress-report.pdf.

American Psychological Association. "Stress: The Different Kinds of Stress." Retrieved August 24, 2016. http://www.apa.org/helpcenter/stress-kinds.aspx.

American Psychological Association. "Understanding Psychotherapy and How It Works." Retrieved October 3, 2016. http://www.apa.org/helpcenter/understanding-psychotherapy.aspx.

Centers for Disease Control and Prevention. "Depression." Mental Health Basics, retrieved October 14, 2016. http://www.cdc.gov/mentalhealth/basics/mental-illness/depression.htm.

Centers for Disease Control and Prevention. "Physical Activity Facts." Healthy Schools, Retrieved October 25, 2016. http://www.cdc.gov/healthyschools/physicalactivity/facts.htm.

Centre for Studies on Human Stress. "Understand Your Stress: Acute vs. Chronic Stress." Retrieved September 28, 2016. http://www.humanstress.ca/stress/understand-your-stress/acute-vs-chronic-stress.html.

Common Sense Media. "The Common Sense Census: Media Use by Tweens and Teens." Retrieved October 8, 2016. http://static1.1.sqspcdn.com/static/f/1083077/26645197/1446492628567/CSM_TeenTween_MediaCensus_FinalWebVersion_1.pdf?token=DyqCzLrJhC4AG9hCITczCD9uJyE%3D.

Mayo Clinic. "Teen Depression." Retrieved September 15, 2016. http://www.mayoclinic.org/diseases-conditions/teen-depression/symptoms-causes/dxc-20164556.

National Institute on Drug Abuse for Teens. "Brain and Addiction." National Institute on Drug Abuse, Retrieved October 4, 2016. https://teens.drugabuse.gov/drug-facts/brain-and-addiction.

National Institute of Mental Health. "Depression." Retrieved October 13, 2016. https://www.nimh.nih.gov/health/topics/depression/index.shtml.

National Institute of Mental Health. "Teen Depression." Retrieved October 13, 2016. https://www.nimh.nih.gov/health/publications/teen-depression/index.shtml.

National Sleep Foundation. "Teens and Sleep." Retrieved October 8, 2016. https://sleepfoundation.org/sleep-topics/teens-and-sleep.

Office of Disease Prevention and Health Promotion. "2016 United States Report Card on Physical Activity for Children and Youth Released." November 16, 2016. https://health.gov/news/blog-bayw/2016/11/2016-united-states-report-card-on-physical-activity-for-children-and-youth-released.

Pew Research Center. "Teens, Social Media & Technology Overview 2015." Retrieved October 4, 2016. http://www.pewinternet.org/2015/04/09/teens-social-media-technology-2015.

Shute, Nancy. "Pediatricians Say School Should Start Later for Teens' Health." NPR, August 25, 2014. http://www.npr.org/sections/health-shots/2014/08/25/343125751/pediatricians-say-school-should-start-later-for-teens-health.

Teens Health. "Alcohol." Nemours, retrieved November 2, 2016. http://kidshealth.org/en/teens/alcohol.html#catdrugs.

U.S. Department of Health and Human Services. "A Day in the Life." Retrieved October 12, 2016. http://www.hhs.gov/ash/oah/adolescent-health-topics/americas-adolescents/day.html.

U.S. Department of Health and Human Services, National Institutes of Health, National Institute of Mental Health. Depression (NIH Publication No. 15-3561). Bethesda, MD: U.S. Government Printing Office, 2015.

INDEX

A

adrenaline, 9, 54
American Academy of
    Pediatrics, 46
American Psychological
    Association (APA), 4, 39

B

Bell Jar, The, 19
bipolar disorder, 26
bullying, 6, 14–15, 25, 29

C

Centers for Disease Control
    and Prevention (CDC), 36
Centre for Studies on Human
    Stress, 11
chronic stress, 6, 11, 16, 34, 49
comfort food, 37–38
coping mechanisms, 42
cortisol, 9

D

depression,
    causes of, 21–25
    definition of, 19–21
    symptoms of, 25–28, 34–39
    treatment of, 48–51
    trauma, 25

Depression Toolbox, 49
drug abuse, 36–37
DSM-V, 26

E

Erika's Lighthouse, 49
exercise, 44, 50

F

fight-or-flight response, 9

G

genetics, 6, 21, 26, 49

H

home life, 16–17
hormones, 6, 8–9, 15, 23, 32

L

learning disabilities, 12
LGBTQ people, depression in,
    30
long-term stress, 6, 10–11, 14,
    17, 34, 38, 48

M

major depressive disorder
    (MDD), 26

Mayo Clinic, 9
medication, 16, 22, 26
Mental Health America, 12
multitasking, 18

N

National Institute for Drug
    Abuse (NIDA), 36
National Institute of Mental
    Health (NIMH), 19
National Physical Activity Plan
    Alliance, 44
National Sleep Foundation, 43
nature vs. nurture, 21–25
neurotransmitters, 22

O

overeating, 37–38

P

peers, 15
Persistent Depressive Disorder
    (PDD), 26
Plath, Sylvia, 19, 20

S

school, 5, 12–15, 17, 20, 24,
    40, 41, 43, 46, 48
seasonal affective disorder
    (SAD), 26
self-harm, 20, 28, 39
Selye, Hans, 8–9

setting priorities, 45–48
sleep, 4, 14, 28, 33, 43, 44
social media, 4, 14, 17, 18, 41
stigma, 28–29
stress
    good and bad, 10
    management of, 42–48
    research on, 8–12
    severity of, 10–12
    stressors, 5, 6, 13–18, 35, 49
    symptoms of, 32–34
stress management, 42–48
stressors, 5, 6, 13–18, 35, 49
Stress Screener, 12
suicide, 28, 39
support network, 51
sympathetic nervous system
    (SNS), 9

T

technology, 14, 17, 44
temporary stress, 6, 16, 20
time management, 18
trauma, 14, 25
trigger, 6, 10, 13, 25, 35

U

United States Report Card on
    Physical Activity for Children
    and Youth, 44

ABOUT THE AUTHOR

Sabrina Parys is a writer and editor living in Brooklyn, New York. She enjoys working with and writing about mental health topics for young adults and teens. Her guide on eating disorders, *Helping a Friend with an Eating Disorder*, was published by Rosen Publishing in 2017.

PHOTO CREDITS

Cover, p. 11 Sabphoto/Shutterstock.com, p. 5 Digital Vision/ Getty Images; pp. 8, 19, 32, 42 chuanpis/Shutterstock.com; p. 9 Bettmann/Getty Images; p. 15 ColorBlind Images/The Image Bank/Getty Images; p. 16 Viosin/Phanie/Canopy/ Getty Images; p. 18 Steve Prezant/Image Source/Getty Images; p. 20 Photo Researchers/Science Source/Getty Images; p. 22 JGI/Jamie Grill/Blend Images/Getty Images; p. 24 Andrew Olney/Stockbyte/Getty Images; p. 27 sturdi/ E+/Getty Images; p. 30 Peter Cade/The Image Bank/ Getty Images; p. 33 Kaspars Grinvalds/Shutterstock.com; p. 35 Thomas Grass/The Image Bank/Getty Images; p. 37 © iStockphoto.com/posteriori; p. 38 Lihee Avidan/ Photonica World/Getty Images; p. 43 Monkey Business Images/Shutterstock.com; p. 45 Sasa Prudkov/ Shutterstock.com; p. 47 PeopleImages/DigitalVision/Getty Images; p. 50 track5/E+/Getty Images; back cover photo by marianna armata/Moment/Getty Images.

Design: Michael Moy; Layout Design: Tahara Anderson; Editor: Bernadette Davis; Photo Researcher: Nicole Baker